...tock...tick...tock...tick...tock...tick...tock...tick...tock...tick...tock...tick...tock...tick...tock...

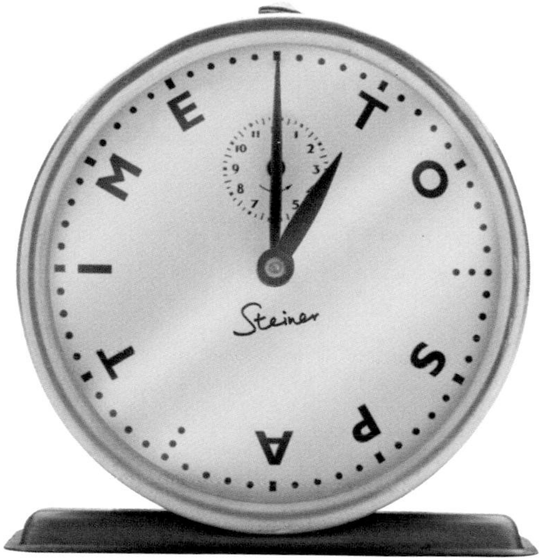
TIME TO SPA
Steiner

Library of Congress Cataloging-in Publication Data Steiner Management Services LLC. Time to Spa.

Published by Steiner Management Services LLC, a division of Steiner Leisure Ltd., 770 South Dixie Highway, Suite 200, Coral Gables, Florida 33146

President and Publisher: Leonard Fluxman

Editor: Sarah Jacob Walker

Copy Editor: Monica Pollans

Art Director: Sally Ann Field

Photography: Wes Bender / pages 19, 20, 22, 30, 45, 50, 65, 69, 78, 86. Louis Jay / page 4. Philip John / cover and pages 32, 38, 61, 66, 74. Elemis Ltd. / pages 37, 39. St. Gregory Java Spa in Singapore / page 42. All other images ©PhotoDisc.

A catalogue record for this book is available from the National Library of USA ISBN 0-96770400-0-6

Steiner Leisure Ltd. owns Steiner Transocean Ltd., the spa operator on board over one hundred cruise ships and Steiner Spa Resorts which helps design and operate spas on land. Steiner Leisure Ltd. also owns Elemis Ltd, the manufacturer and distributor of Elemis, an established aromatherapy brand of skin care products available in destination spas and day spas throughout Great Britain, on board cruise ships and the Orient. Steiner Leisure Ltd. also owns accredited post secondary educational schools teaching the art of massage, facial therapy and acupuncture in the United States of America.

The Publisher would like to thank the following who contributed much of the information contained within this book: Noella Gabrielle, Aromatherapist for Elemis Ltd., Dr. He, Doctor of Acupuncture and Herbology, Barbara Mazulli, Registered Facial Specialist and Margie Meshew, Licensed Massage Therapist – all teaching at the Florida College of Natural Health. We would also like to thank Dr. Deborah Sarnoff, private practicing Dermatologist and Assistant Clinical Professor at New York University. Finally, a special thank you to all the Steiner beauty therapists, fitness instructors, yoga instructors and Reiki practitioners who between them have at least 1000 years of "spa" experience.

Note from the Publisher: This book is not intended as a medical reference book. Readers are not advised to attempt self treatment, nor to embark upon a detoxification program or exercise regime without first consulting a qualified expert. The Publisher can not be held responsible for any adverse reaction to the recommendations and instructions contained within this book.

When we asked both men and women if they ever spent "time" with themselves we got a few strange looks. "Of course I spend time with myself," giggled one woman, "... I can't get away from myself," she continued jovially. All our interviewees missed the point entirely. We had to be more explicit with our questioning. We rephrased: "Do you ever spend time doing things for yourself like dipping in a hot, aromatic bath or meditating?" "Do you ever turn out the lights, unplug the phone and think about nothing?" Our interviewees stopped laughing at this point and some looked a little guilty," ... I always intend to, but there just never seems to be time." This is the common complaint of all of us, including myself who juggles career with family and other "necessities." And we are so "busy" that we don't even question the way we fill our days. When exactly was it, that old Father Time became the enemy? When did we schedule our life with "busy-ness?" When did self-cultivation and self-awareness become less important than all the other extraneous events and quests that steal away all that beautiful, ephemeral time?

We know that there is still an extravagance associated with visiting a spa. Many of our customers, both on board cruise ships and in our land based spas, have their first spa experience with us. They most commonly book in for an aromatic full body massage. For many their second massage will be on their next vacation in six to twelve months time. Why? Because spending a couple of hours relaxing on a massage bed or in a thalassotherapy pool sounds so utterly luxurious. It sounds almost, dare I say, like the epitome of "time wasted." It seems unproductive. But what if self-cultivation became a priority? What if health and well being were primary elements in your life? What if you decided that there is a connection between well-being, self awareness and quality of life? Then surely, adopting a spa lifestyle within your own financial means, would not be an extravagance. It would be an absolute necessity. It would be the time to spa now. Right now.

Our conclusion is this. By creating time to spa, you will become more self aware, you will enhance your well being, and be more productive. There is time for everything. Including you. This book, "Time to Spa," serves as a reminder and a guide for living well. It is a celebration of the individual and has been created to inspire you to care for yourself from top to toe. Both Steiner and Elemis know the secrets of wellbeing. It's time to share them with you, our customers. What are you waiting for? It's time to spa.

Sarah Jacob Walker, Editor

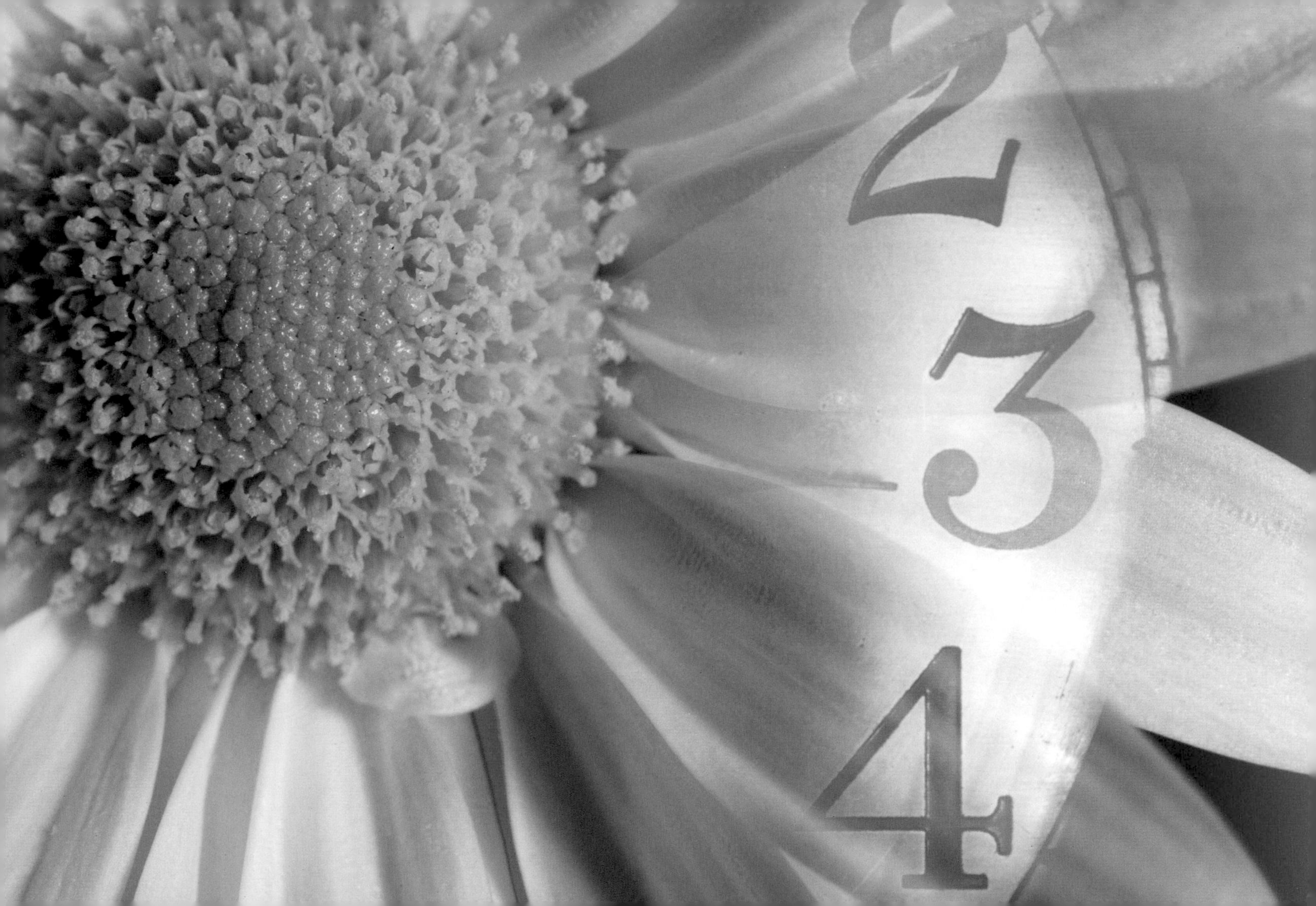
2
3
4

time This man-made phenomenon makes us squeeze beautiful moments into square boxes. We try to beat the clock and pack our twelve-hour days with purpose and meaning. We try to stop. We try to do nothing. But old cultural myths creep into our psyche, like a whispering mantra, "Idle hands are the devil's workshop." Yet we continue going through life, measuring our progress by a round object that hangs upon a wall and ticks. Time terrifies us. Henri Bergson, a French philosopher born upon the cusp of the 19th and 20th centuries, re-invented time. He proposed that real time was the "inner" time of experience. He called it "La Durée." Immeasurable and purely qualitative, it never begins and never ends. It is the constant event of becoming. It is the immortal moment. Time flows, it does not tick and when experienced as such it is the vehicle for self discovery. Take time. Face time. **Enjoy your time.**

We need time to dream, time to remember, and time to reach the infinite. Time to be.

GLADYS TABER, 20TH CENTURY AMERICAN WRITER

what's inside

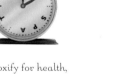

Time for East

What is Yin and Yang?
Learn about some
Eastern delights like Reiki,
Shiatsu and Yoga.

Time to Meditate

What is meditation?
Try using our
meditation guide.

Time for Water

What are the healing
properties of water?
Find out why a day at the beach
is health provoking.

Time for Exercise

Learn some unconventional
ways to burn off calories and
get a cardiovascular workout.

Changing the Face of Time

What is the difference
between intrinsic aging
and extrinsic aging?
Find out how
to eat yourself young!

Stress...the black metal ball that sits in your stomach...

the frantic re-thinking of overthought, thoughts...the grim reaper of youth and joy...

the trouble maker of the modern world.

1

Time to De-Stress

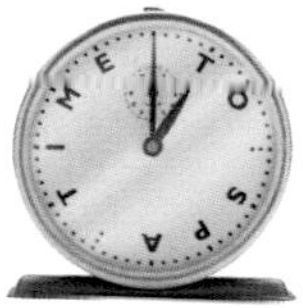
TIME TO SPA

Stress is the "buzzword." Everyone knows how stress feels, but not many know exactly what happens in the body when it is "stressed" or, even more importantly, how to cope with it. According to research, stress-related diseases in the United States of America exceeds $100 billion a year. This is attributed to health care costs, lost productivity, and absenteeism.[1] In other words, stress is a modern disease, which needs to be dealt with by each individual accordingly. The good news is that before stress controls you, you can control it by adopting some healthy lifestyle changes.

In the United States, stress-related diseases cost over $100 billion a year.

So, what exactly is stress? Quite simply it is your body's (including psychological, physical and emotional) response to a new situation. According to Margie Meshew, Massage Teacher at Florida College of Natural Health, when the body responds to "stress," the sympathetic nervous system is alerted to prepare the body for a shock. Often this is referred to as the "fight" or "flight" system. Adrenaline is increased giving the body extra strength to fight or run, the heart rate increases, the pupils dilate, the palms become sweaty and the brain is completely alert. Many chemicals are produced in the body in preparation for the "stressor." When the threatening situation is over, the para-sympathetic nervous system takes over. This slows down the blood pressure and reverses the work done by the sympathetic nervous system, calming the entire mind and body down. However, during these bodily events, "'metabolic" waste is created, (in the animal kingdom this would be used up by either running or fighting) which is considered toxic.

It is necessary to release these toxins from the body, in order to eliminate the effect that stress could have upon health. It is important to note that in the technological and commercial world in which we live, there are many stressors that occur on a daily basis. These could be as simple as being late for an appointment, missing a train, having to meet deadlines, public speaking, or more dramatically, escaping a life threatening situation. The body responds to all stressors in a similar fashion—producing metabolic waste, which needs to be expelled from the body. Creating time to spa will help lessen the effect that stress can have in your life.

Lessen the Stress. Jog, jump, run, swim. Energetically banish the stress build up from your body. Have a massage every week. Give your partner a massage every week. Inhale aromatherapy essential oils. Spend ten minutes a day breathing deeply. Work in the garden, plant your own veggies and flowers. Do something to save the planet. Go on a beach walk. Let the water splash on your bare feet. Enjoy the wind in your hair. Say "no" when you want to. Say "yes" and really mean it. Give someone you love a bear hug. Cuddle a furry friend. Enjoy being naked more often. Have a pillow fight. Laugh your head off. Fall asleep under the stars. Smile at the sky.

Never eat more   than you can lift.

MISS PIGGY

12345678910

Time to Detox

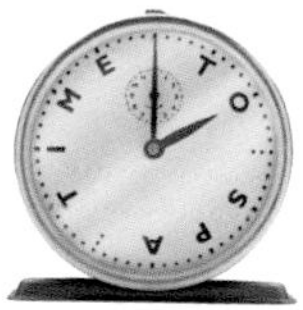
TIME TO SPA

Detoxification is Ancient

Most of the oldest religions include a yearly cleansing ritual that aids detoxification through some form of fasting. While the reasons for this may be explained religiously, it cannot be missed that fasting is a very healthy ritual for the mind, body and soul. There is value in the process of detoxification, not only for spiritual health, but also physical and psychological health. You are removing poisons from your body, which will increase physical energy and also benefit the psyche by evoking a positive state of mind. The old sages that preached these yearly detoxification rituals had a great advantage over us. They were much closer to nature; they had no processed foods; pesticides, artificial colorants or flavorings were not used on their foods; their cattle were not raised on hormones; the stress in their lives was completely related to "danger." The list of cultural differences is endless. While a yearly fasting ritual was adequate detoxification for them, for us it is vital that we eat consciously every day ensuring that fresh and natural foods are part of our lifestyle.

Detoxifying Your Body for Well-Being and Beauty

Your body will tell you when it needs detoxifying. One of the signs is fatigue and lethargy and a general sense of feeling "under the weather." A slow circulation also minimizes the elimination of the toxins from the body. This in turn, can lead to a toxin build up that inhibits proper absorption of vital nutrients needed for health and vitality. In recent years, "cellulite" has been labeled the single most distressing result of toxin build-up and, with the help of the media, more and more people are growing excessively self conscious about this type of fat. In the cosmetics industry, Cellulite is the term used for the appearance of puckered skin around the fatty areas, like the thighs and buttocks. It is most common, but not limited to, overweight women and those with both a slow circulation and slow metabolism. At some stage in your life you may experience cellulite, and if you do, remember it is completely normal. For some, cellulite is inherited through genetics and for others it is provoked through lifestyle choices. For most of us it is a combination of both. The appearance of cellulite can be "smoothed," but complete elimination is rare. The most effective way to smooth the appearance of cellulite is by reducing your "toxin" intake and embarking upon an active, healthful lifestyle. In other words, by making time to spa. The following pages offer some healthy tips.

THE FRUIT FAST

Every couple of months do the "fruit fast" over a two day weekend. You must plan it for a weekend when you have no obligations or commitments. It cannot be on a weekend booked up with socializing or shopping. You don't have to do "nothing." You can do light exercise like walking, gardening or reading a good book. Make use of this weekend – get your pharmacy of face, body oils lotions and essential oils, along with relaxation music and meditation techniques to accompany you through the fruit fast.

Foods you will need: Fruits of all kinds. **Water.** Herbal Teas.

For the entire weekend you will eat fruit only. Do not overload on citrus fruit – the acid may make you feel sick, but strawberries, bananas, pears, grapes, cherries etc. – can be eaten without much caution. Wash the fruit down with herbal tea. If you need sweetener then add natural honey. Relax. This is time for you so do some things you never have time for normally, like writing, reading, taking an aromatic bath or meditating.

Note: Wherever possible, eat organic fruit and teas. Healthy people should be able to 'fruit fast' for two days without any adverse effects. Do not fruit fast if you have to work or do tasks that require focus. You may feel slightly tired, get a slight headache or just feel like you have no energy. We recommend you consult a healthcare professional before trying the fruit fast. Do not fruit fast if you are pregnant, breast feeding or are taking medication.

Toxin Builders

Saturated fats, alcohol, artificial ingredients, smoking, caffeine, stress and pollution in the environment add to the build up of toxins in the body. Most people consume a lot of toxins in a single day, the excess of which, need to be released from the body. Some of the more "radical" detox diets suggest the only answer is a completely natural Vegan diet. This eliminates everything apart from fresh fruits and veggies, legume's, beans, grains and pulses. However, for most of us, a sudden change in our diet terrifies us. We like what we eat. While the ideal detox diet eliminates all toxin builders, the key to success is "baby steps." Do what you can. Cut down on toxin builders. Change your attitude. Do not think of these "toxin" builders as "vices." Eating junk food, like smoking and drinking is just a "learned" habit—a bad habit you have learned to enjoy. The real secret to successful detoxification is the slow re-education of your tastebuds and lifestyle. This is a process that will take time and concentration because you cannot change your lifestyle instantaneously.

Cut out or cut down on: All meat especially red and processed meat. Junk foods like chips, fries and pastries. Foods with artificial flavorings and colorings. Food with high sodium. Alcohol. Smoking.

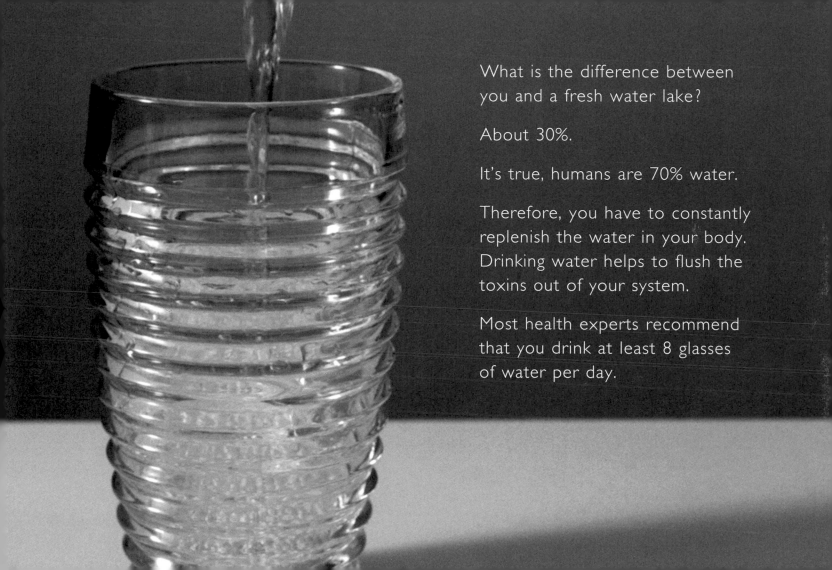

What is the difference between you and a fresh water lake?

About 30%.

It's true, humans are 70% water.

Therefore, you have to constantly replenish the water in your body. Drinking water helps to flush the toxins out of your system.

Most health experts recommend that you drink at least 8 glasses of water per day.

LITTLE DETOXIFICATION HELPERS

Water Drinking water helps to flush your system. Most health experts recommend you to drink 8 glasses of water per day. Tip: Every morning drink some hot water and lemon to cleanse your inner body. **Dry Skin Brush** Use a bristle brush (not synthetic) to brush the body. Brush upwards from the soles of the feet towards the heart everyday before your shower. Brushing the body removes dry skin cells, improves the circulation and helps to eliminate toxins. Do this ritual morning and night. **Enjoy** saunas, steam or thermal baths once or twice a week. **Thalassotherapy Pools** Filled with bubbling thalassotherapy seawater, these pools help the body detoxify and improve sluggish metabolisms. **Hydrotherapy Spa Baths** The heat along with a combination of detoxifying essential oils like Juniper and Rosemary, or pure seaweed can help the body to eliminate toxins. **Massage** Often stiff and sore joints are the result of a build up of toxins. Swedish massage (see page 36) helps to drain the impurities out of the body through the lymphatic system. **Seaweed Treatments** Seaweed helps the body to detoxify because it is full of minerals and iodine. Concentrated seaweed treatments like the Elemis Aromaspa therapy help to drain the toxins from the body. **Swimming in the Ocean** It's not a pure co-incidence that you feel energized when you plunge into the ocean. Iodine and minerals in the seawater help boost the metabolism, which like the Thalassotherapy pool, helps to eliminate toxins from the body. **Go for Green** Foods high in anti-oxidants are naturally detoxifying. Eat greens and fruits – as much fresh, organic food as possible. **Breathe** Read the next chapter to learn how to breathe properly. **Detoxification Herbs** Alterative herbs at one time were known as "blood cleansers." These include Bladderwrack, Blue Flag, Bogbean, Burdock, Cleavers, Echinacea, Red Clover, Sarasarilla, Yellow Dock and Diuretic herbs like Saw Palmetto, Parsley, Dandelion, Hawthorn Berries also help to drain toxins from the body. **Detox Tea** Dry your own Cleavers. Grind the dried leaves and then use two teaspoons in a cup of boiling water. Let your tea brew for ten minutes. Enjoy a cup, two or three times a day.

Note: If you are pregnant do not use herbs, aromatherapy or attempt to detox without your doctors supervision and recommendation.

"Perfect simplicity is unconsciously audacious."

GEORGE MEREDITH, 19TH CENTURY ENGLISH POET

"Health is a state of complete physical, mental and social well-being, and not merely the absence of disease or infirmity." WORLD HEALTH ORGANIZATION: CONSTITUTION, 1948

12345678910

Time to Breathe

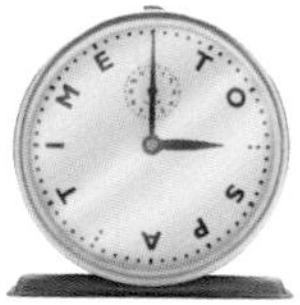
TIME TO SPA

Breathing is an art these days. Something that is so natural has been forgotten. Thousands of years ago, the breath was seen as sacred. It was the symbol of life itself. But today, as we dash from one venue to the next, our breathing is rapid and shallow. However, breathing, when done properly, can energize you, help to detoxify your body, slow your heart rate and improve a sluggish metabolism. Breathing correctly is the key to maximizing your energy levels. All these benefits are yours for free if you just take the time to breathe. The reason that breathing properly is so beneficial is because a deep breath transports oxygen around the body more efficiently, to all the vital organs, the blood cells and skin tissue. For these reasons try and make slow, deep abdominal breathing part of a daily exercise.

If you watch a baby breathe you will note that the breath expands the entire abdomen. This abdominal breath is natural to us and it is what these breathing techniques will help you to re-learn. Like the baby, inhale right down into the abdomen. Your tummy should push out as you inhale, and go completely flat as you exhale. If you are not sure if you are doing it correctly, lie down and place your book on your abdomen. The book should rise as you breathe in, and fall as you breathe out. Once you have mastered the art, resume a comfortable sitting position. Your back should be straight. Drop your shoulders. Practice this abdominal breath slowly, without strain, ten times. Experience the oxygen as it travels through your nose, down your wind-pipe, into your lungs and around your body. Visualization techniques can help to enhance the positive effect of breathing. As you breathe out, you can visualize all the negative energy being released from your body looking like a cloud of smoke; as you breathe in, you can visualize a bright light, a symbol of purity entering your body, cleansing your entire system. We recommend you do three sets of ten abdominal breaths a day. Adjust the breath to your own rhythm.

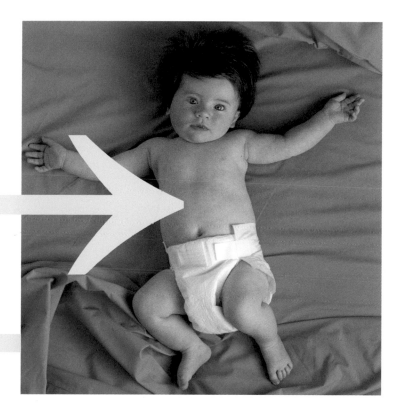

"Healing, Papa would tell me, is not a science,
but the intuitive art of wooing 'Nature.'"

W.H. AUDEN, THE ART OF HEALING, 20TH CENTURY AMERICAN POET

4 Time for Aromatherapy

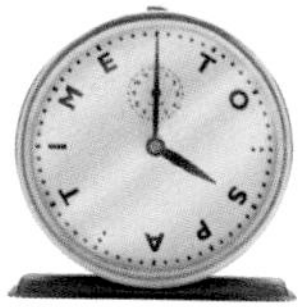
TIME TO SPA

Flowers with Power

Plants have been known to have healing powers since the dawn of mankind. In their flowers, seeds, roots, leaves or bark—the secrets of life or death are locked, healing, or harmful, depending on how they are used. Shamans or witch doctors would help heal entire communities with a mixture of plants and magic since ancient times. In the years between 3000 BCE and 1500 BCE, herbal essences were in common use both as medicinal aids and body beautifiers. Egyptian priests used such herbs as Camphor, Spikehard, Saffron, Calamus, Cinnamon, Frankincense, Myrrh and Aloes—all of which are still used today. The interest in and use of herbal medicines began to ebb in the 18th and 19th century with the advent of modern medicine.

The Revival

After World War II, an aromatic renaissance began to blossom. By the sixties, this return to nature was flourishing and aromatherapy had made a huge come back. Gattefosse, a French chemist, wrote a book called "Aromatherapie" and researched the effect of aromatherapy as a cure for skin cancer, burns and chronic wounds. His work was continued by Dr. Jean Valnet who treated war wounds with aromatherapy and documented positive results. He also wrote a book called "Aromatherapie" in 1964 and it is thanks to him that Aromatherapy gained acceptance as a beneficial treatment.

"Learn what you are and be such. PINDAR, ODES (5TH CENTURY B.C.)

So What is Aromatherapy?

Quite simply, it is a beneficial treatment using the essential oil of plants, bark, roots and flowers. Aromatherapy is considered "holistic" therapy. It treats the cause of a symptom and includes the emotional, physical and psychological aspects of a person. The aroma can be inhaled into the blood stream or absorbed through carrier oils helping to heal emotional, mental and physical destress. In the hierarchy of sense perception, your sense of smell is the third most acute. It is 10,000 times more aware than that of touch and taste. An aroma can stimulate part of the brain to release hormones and neurochemicals that can actually alter human behavior. Peter and Kate Damian, authors of the book "Aromatherapy Scent and Psyche," note that in the University of Cincinnati, a study showed that fragrances of peppermint and lily of the valley increased subjects' performance accuracy by 15 to 25%. Each essential oil has a different physical, therapeutic and psychological function.

Essential oils are a plant's life blood. It is a vital, living force.

Dismiss the romantic myth of nature. Nature can be beautiful and healthful. But, it is also powerful and can be deadly. Do not think that because something is natural it cannot harm you. Nature is paradoxical. It heals and harms, so you must approach natural remedies with caution and with guidance from an aromatherapist.

	Eucalyptus	Rosemary	Rosewood	Lemon	Chamomile	Ylang Ylang
	Eucalyptus Globulus	Rosmarinus Officinalis	Aniba Rosaedora	Citrus Limonum	Anthemis Mixta	Canagium Oderatum
therapy	The solution for runny noses. Helps clear sinuses and respiratory system.	General stimulant.	Calming and soothing.	Gives you a new zest for life. Stimulates the senses.	Calms and soothes inflamed skin. Helps relieve cystitis.	Helps to relax and encourage inner calm.
mind	Revitalizes, soothes and comforts.	Relieves mental strain and fatigue. Helps prompt the memory. Use before making important decisions.	For those run down days. Provokes feeling of euphoria, uplifts the spirits.	Refreshes and invigorates. Lemon helps clear the mind encouraging sharp thinking.	Evokes peace of mind. Anti-depressant, helps combat insomnia and calms irritability.	The love potion. Calms anger, provokes a state of euphoria and a as an aphrodisia
tip	Add a few drops to a sauna, put on a handkerchief or pillow when you have a cold.	Pour a few drops in a bath or inhale the essence by adding a few drops to Elemis Fragrancer.	Use in Elemis Fragrancer or in the bath to aid meditation.	Pour a few drops on a handkerchief or in Elemis Fragrancer before important meetings or exams.	Add a few drops with Eucalyptus to your Elemis Fragrancer to help relieve hayfever.	Known as the flower of flowers Let the aroma ign romance during a candlelit dinner
synergy	Mix Eucalyptus and Lemon to wake up your whole system.	Blends well with Juniper.	Blends well with Ylang Ylang.	Blends well with Lavender, Ylang Ylang and Sandalwood.	Blends well with Lavender, Ylang Ylang and Geranium.	Blends well with Sandalwood, Gerar and Chamomile

"Nothing awakens a reminiscence like an odour."

Lavender	Geranium	Juniper	Sandalwood	Lime	Tea Tree	
LAVANDULA OFFICINALIS	PELARGONIUM ROSEUM X ASPERUM	JUNIPERUS COMMUNIS	SANTALUM ALBUM	CITRUS MEDICA	MELALEUCA ALTERNIFOLIA	
Helps heal scars, minimize stretch marks soothes insect bites. Encourages sleep.	Stimulates the adrenal cortex and is an effective astringent.	Detox and body cleanser. Reduces muscle pain and acts as a diuretic. Purifying.	Calming, balancing and stimulating.	Stimulates the mind and acts as an uplifting tonic.	Natures own antiseptic, disinfects and acts as a first aid oil.	therapy
The stress buster, Helps to balance energy, de-stresses and soothes.	Uplifts, balances anxiety and eases nervous tension.	Stimulates the mind.	Musky, rich and exotic. Use as a meditation aid and aphrodisiac.	Get fresh – refreshes the mind and encourages fearless optimism.	Uplifts the spirits.	mind
Add to a bath, relax as your troubles dissolve. Use in Elemis Fragrancer to evoke sweet slumber.	Called the "female essential oil." Use during pre-menstrual tension and menopause.	Use in the bath and in Elemis Fragrancer as part of your detox program.	Let the aroma fill the room in an Elemis Fragrancer or sprinkle a few drops in your bath.	Freshen the aroma of your home with a few drops of lime in your Elemis Fragrancer.	Use on compresses or in bath. Use to disinfect body brushes or sponges.	tip
Blends well with Geranium, Eucalyptus and Juniper.	Blends well with Lavender and Lemon.	Blends well with Rosemary.	Blends well with Lemon.	Blends well with Juniper.	Blends well with Eucalyptus and Rosemary.	synergy

Body Cleansing Massage Oil

20 ml of Elemis Japanese Camellia Oil

or Evening Primrose Oil

2-3 drops of Juniper Essential Oil

2-3 drops of Rosemary Essential Oil

Use every night after your shower. Massage the Body Cleansing Massage Oil into the thighs and buttocks. If you suffer from water retention, massage it into effected areas. Pour 15 drops of the mixture to a running bath.

Mixing your own potions. Although it is always advisable to have your oils mixed by a professional, there is nothing to stop you from mixing your own oils at home as long as you remember to be responsible. Remember, essential oils are powerful, so if you increase the recommended amount of drops of essential oils you include in a carrier oil or in your bath, you could burn your skin or have an allergic reaction. Respect the power of the oils and handle with care.

Essentially for you. Not all essential oils are for you. This is why aromatherapists insist upon giving each client a proper consultation. However, it is good signal that an oil will be of benefit to you if you like the smell. Follow your nose.

YOUR MIXING KIT SHOULD INCLUDE: A plastic bowl, measuring spoon and a couple of hours. Use your measuring spoon to pour 20 ml of the Evening Primrose or Camellia Oil in a plastic bowl. Pour in the drops of essential oil and mix it all together with the spoon. 20 ml will be enough for one or two full body applications.

Note: If you are pregnant or breast feeding do not use essential oils. Elemis pre-mixes many bath oils and massage oils and it is recommended that you do use a pre-mixed oil as opposed to mixing your own. However, if the curious spirit gets the better of you, at least make sure you follow our strict guidelines.

Oil for Insomniacs

20 ml of Elemis Japanese Camellia Oil
or Evening Primrose Oil
2-3 drops of Lavender Essential Oil
2-3 drops of Chamomile Essential Oil

Lavender and Chamomile are perhaps the two most popular essential oils and are used in many skin care potions. Either massage the mixture into your body or pour 15 drops in the bath. Either way, you should be able to calm your nerves, reduce your stress and enjoy a wonderful night of peaceful slumber.

Woman's Oil

20 ml of Elemis Japanese Camellia Oil
or Evening Primrose Oil
2-3 drops of Geranium Essential Oil
2-3 drops of Ylang Ylang Essential Oil

Use whenever you are suffering from pre-menstrual tension. Pour some of this mixture into the palm of your hand and massage your body. The potion helps evoke a feeling of euphoria while gently relaxing the mind and body. You can either ask your partner to massage you or you can try self massage. Alternatively, pour 15 drops in a bath, close your eyes and let all the tension dissolve.

Decongesting Massage Oils

20 ml of Elemis Japanese Camellia Oil
or Evening Primrose Oil
2-3 drops of Tea Tree Essential Oil
2-3 drops of Eucalyptus Essential Oil

Massage into the chest. Alternative use: pour a few drops of undiluted Eucalyptus essential oil and Tea Tree essential oil on to your pillow or handkerchief and inhale during the night, or fill a pan full of boiling water and pour in a few drops of each oil. Let the aroma fill your room. The aroma will soon help unblock your sinuses.

"The essence of pleasure is spontaneity.

GERMAINE GREER, 20TH CENTURY AUSTRALIAN WRITER AND FEMINIST

Time for Massage

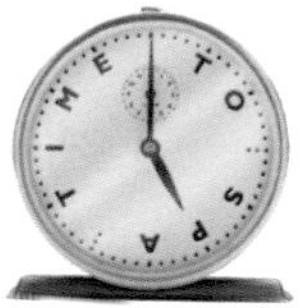
TIME TO SPA

Like aromatherapy, massage has been used for its holistic health benefits.

Even the medical profession recognizes massage as having curative value. It definitely helps to relieve "stress," one of the largest contributors to ill-health in the Western World. Massage cannot "cure" stress related illnesses, but it can help to eliminate the "metabolic waste" created by stress from the body. Professional massage therapists agree that regular massage treatments can prevent stress from burgeoning into more complicated illnesses. Massage works with the para-sympathetic nervous system helping to completely calm the emotional, physical and psychological aspects of the body. According to experts, there are some biological events that take place in the body during a massage: the lymphatic flow is increased which stimulates the elimination of toxins from the body; the blood flow is increased improving the circulation; and the blood pressure and heart rate is decreased. How does this translate to you? Common stress related symptoms like insomnia, irritability, anxiety, depression and the inability to concentrate can be lessened and often eliminated by making the time to enjoy a regular massage.

MASSAGE TO STOP SMOKING

According to a study done by the Touch Research Institute, the anxiety, stress and bad moods caused by cigarette craving were greatly reduced when the study group practiced self massage. According to the article, the treatment group was taught to conduct a hand or ear self-massage during three cravings a day for one month. This resulted in lower anxiety scores, improved mood and fewer withdrawal symptoms.[2]

Holistic therapists agree that every aspect of a person is connected. Emotional upsets beget physical ailments and physical ailments have a bearing upon mental and emotional health. It sounds so simple, but more often we treat emotional anxiety as being something completely unrelated to physical health, and physical problems as having nothing to do with our state of mind. According to holistic therapy, healing will take place when we recognize that any effect upon the psyche or the body is like a pebble that has been thrown in a pond—the ripple of which will have some bearing upon all aspects of a human being.

Swedish Massage

This is perhaps the most popular massage in the West. It is a deep penetrating massage that helps to stimulate circulation and relieve muscular aches. The massage techniques used are effleurage, pettrisage, tapotement, friction and sometimes range of motion. *Effleurage* is a gentle stroking movement that helps to relax the sensory nerve endings. *Pettrisage* is a deeper kneading movement. This helps to relieve muscular tension by breaking down toxic waste in the muscles. *Tapotement* is a heavier hacking, cupping and pinching movement, which increases circulation and also aids in the removal of toxic wastes through the lymphatic drainage system. *Friction* is a deep movement that creates heat and helps to break down tension. *Range of Motion* is the complete movement of a joint, like the ankle or the arm. This simple motion helps to ease stiff joints by helping pump "synovial" fluid into the joints, keeping the bones lubricated. Swedish massage can be done as frequently as you like but should be done at least monthly and more if there are muscular problems. A "full body" massage includes back, neck, shoulders, full leg, feet, arms and hands and decolette.

Sports Massage

Sports Massage Therapy is also known as "Deep Tissue Massage" and is specifically for those who often strain muscles through physical activity. Excessive stress on the muscles can cause adhesions or "knots" in the tissue and an excessive production of Lactic Acid. This causes a tightening of the muscles which can be very painful. The Sports Massage therapy helps to break down the knots that are in the muscles and also drains away the Lactic Acid. Sports massage is often recommended immediately after a sports injury. One session normally lasts for an hour.

> " It is never too late to be what you might have been. "
>
> GEORGE ELIOT, 19TH CENTURY ENGLISH WRITER

Aromatherapy Massage

Aromatherapy massage uses therapeutic plant extracts to help relieve stress-related concerns like anxiety, tension, headaches and fluid retention, while helping to increase energy levels. All aromatherapists will first consult you either verbally or by using reflexology techniques. In a verbal consultation, you can expect to be asked about your lifestyle including how you view your stress levels, any relaxation techniques you have tried, your diet and nutrition and any areas of concern like fluid retention, insomnia and fatigue. In a consultation using reflexology, the aromatherapists will look at the feet and press different reflexes to determine any stress related concerns (see reflexology, page 46) Following either consultation, specially mixed oils are prepared for your massage.

The Treatment

Aromatherapy massage is a gentle massage with a lot of long, flowing movements to aid in relaxation and the penetration of aromatherapy oils. Lymphatic drainage techniques are used all over the body to assist the drainage of the toxins. It is the most relaxing of the massages and concentrates on the absorption of the oils to aid relaxation holistically. During the massage, Elemis therapists will instruct you to breathe properly, using abdominal breathing (refer to page 23) to further assist the penetration of the essential oils into the blood stream. The main goal of Aromatherapy massage is to help the client release negative energy, which could be causing emotional imbalance, depression and excessive stress.

"Earth's crammed with heaven."

ELIZABETH BARRETT BROWNING, 19TH CENTURY ENGLISH POET

M a s s a g e   Y o u r   P a r t n e r

Your partner's massage experience depends on the entire environment and the mood you evoke.

Atmosphere Ambiance is everything. You should give your partner a massage in an uncluttered space. Dim the lights or work in candlelight. Light a few Elemis burners and pour a few drops of Lavender and Chamomile essential oil mixed with water in the bowl of the burner. Let the aroma flood through your home. Play a soft relaxation CD, depending on your partners mood and state of mind. You can choose from classical to easy listening or new age. Sometimes the best sounds are those of nature, like the ocean and the wind. Unplug your phone.

Remember If you are giving a massage, your posture is very important. Your weight should be balanced, and pressure applied should come from your entire body, not just your wrists. Do not massage bony areas, the kidneys, the spine, bruises or cuts. Always massage towards the heart. You are following the path of the circulation. Always warm the massage oil in your hands before you apply it to the body. Once you have contacted the body with your first massage technique, you must not lose contact until the massage is over. For the first time, a 20-30 minute massage is recommended.

FOUR BASIC MASSAGE MOVEMENT GROUPS

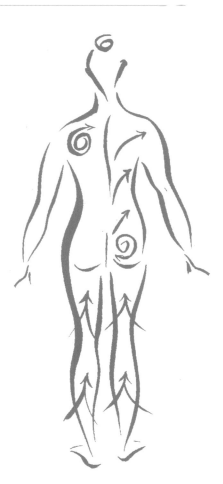

→ Effleurage

This is a stroking movement. It can be either light or deep, as long as it flows. This movement stimulates the circulation. Use both hands and gently stroke the body – one hand following the other, so as not to lose contact.

→ Pettrissage

This is a kneading movement. Just as you would roll and manipulate dough when making bread, this movement allows you to roll and manipulate the muscles. This helps to break down the lactic acid and release toxins from the body.

→ Tapotement

This comprises "hacking," slapping and cupping movements. It helps to increase blood circulation and relax the nerves. It is normally done toward the end of the massage.

→ Friction

This stimulates the circulation and nerve endings. The hands move opposite each other, creating tension and heat, which in turn helps to disperse muscular tension.

Giving your partner a back massage. Start using the effleurage movement and place your hands on either side of the bottom of the spine with your fingers pointing towards the head. Both hands should sweep upwards towards the neck. Remember to avoid applying pressure to the spine itself. Continue the sweeping motion over the shoulders and tops of arms and down either side of the body, returning to the starting position. Start with lighter effleurage movements and then get deeper. Summary of sequence: lower back, neck, shoulders, tops of arms and lightly down the sides of the body. Repeat this sequence twelve times.

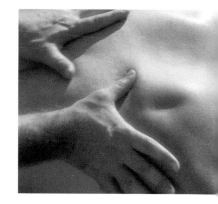

Next, work on one side at a time from the hips to the shoulders, using petrissage. Alternating between your hands, knead the skin, picking up the muscle using the thumb and fingers. Do this 4 times and then repeat on the other side. Return your hands to the base of the spine and lay hands flat on the back, side by side. Alternatively, sweep across the back in a zig zag movement from side to side. Do this all the way up the neck and then all the way back to the base of the spine. Repeat this 4 times. Starting on the right shoulder, pick up the muscles between the fingers and thumbs. Repeat on the left side. Return to the base of the spine using Effleurage either side of the spine to the base of the neck. Starting from the shoulders, stroke downwards with the palm of the hands to the hips. Repeat gentle effleurage movements. Then gently lift your hands away.

"There are two ways of spreading light: to be the candle or the mirror that reflects it." EDITH WHARTON, 19TH / 20TH CENTURY AMERICAN WRITER

6 Time for East

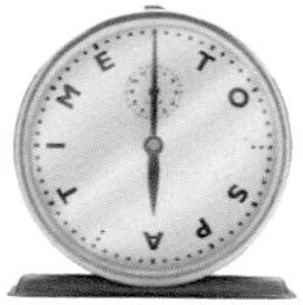
TIME TO SPA

Yin and Yang

All Eastern therapies take into consideration Yin and Yang. These are polar opposites which contain Qi (pronounced Ch'i), commonly translated as energy, in between these two "poles." Yin and Yang are not located in the body, but are present everywhere in the universe. Yin is considered feminine; Yang, masculine. Yin is dark; Yang, light. Yin is passive; Yang, active. Therefore, Yin and Yang are opposing forces which, when balanced, create harmony and when unbalanced, create chaos. The association of Yin and Yang with health necessitates the perfect balance between Yin and Yang in the body for well being. For the Chinese doctor, every ailment, whether it be insomnia, acne, psoriasis or more severe illnesses, is primarily an imbalance of Yin and Yang. The role of Chinese traditional medicine is to restore and sustain the balance between these two poles, and the philosophy of the chinese doctor is not to "cure" a disease, but rather to "prevent" diseases by ensuring Yin and Yang balance.

Qi

Qi is universal energy that flows between Yin and Yang. It is everywhere. The Qi in the body flows through specific pathways called "meridians." These meridians are like threads that carry Qi to every part of the body. Essentially, for the oriental practitioner, it is the life force that flows within and through everything. Sickness is either a misdirection of Qi, or Qi that is blocked.

Yin and Yang are not located in the body, but are present everywhere in the universe.

"Namaste: I honor the spirit in you, which is also in me."

A Nepalese greeting that recognizes the underlying unity in the world

Feet speak. Listen.

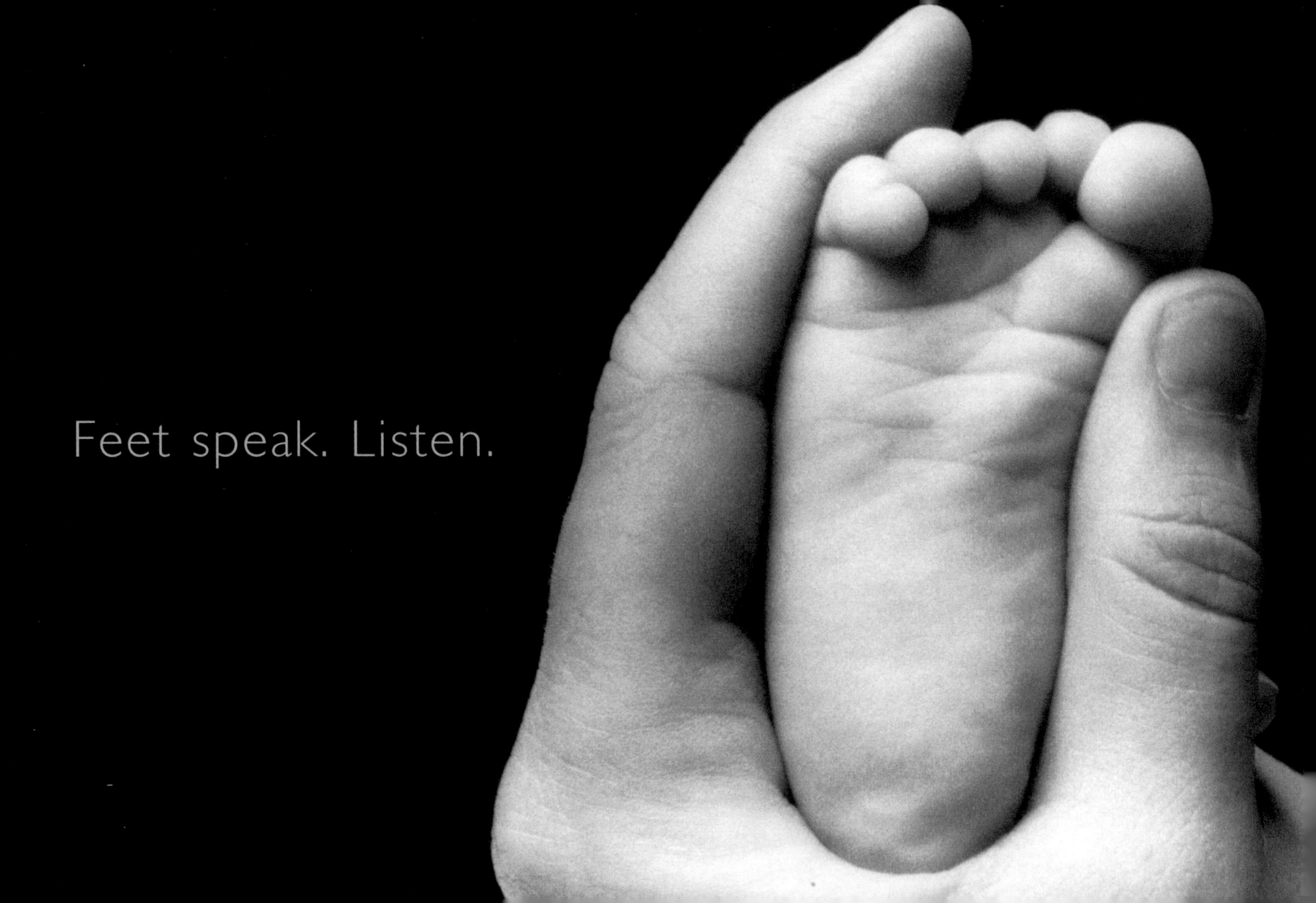

R E F L E X O L O G Y The fundamental theory of reflexology has its roots in the ancient east. However, it only became a therapy of interest early this century when Dr. William Fitzgerald, an American physician, studied the links between the hands and feet with the rest of the body. He found that there were definite links or lines, which are now commonly known as "meridians." There are twelve meridians which are pathways that connect a point in ones hand or foot, all the way to an organ. Following Dr. Fitzgerald's research, Dr. Joseph Shelby Riley recognized the possibilities and furthered the experiments. Soon Eunice Ingram, one of his staff, developed her foot reflexology theory in the 1930's. Her research and case studies gave reflexology some much deserved recognition as an alternative healing therapy.

Philosophy of Reflexology

The soles of the feet and the palms of the hands are mirrors of every organ in the body. Each point on the foot is the ending of a "meridian" or pathway, which is connected to the organ it represents. If the meridian line is blocked or congested, or if there is an irritation in the organ at the end of the meridian, the therapist will feel crystal like formations under the skin. The goal of reflexology is to let the Qi flow freely by pressing on various points on the soles of both feet.

The Treatment

Reflexology techniques can ease stress and unblock Qi by applying pressure to certain points on the soles of the feet. In treatment, the reflexologist normally concentrates on areas on the foot that correspond to the solar plexus for signs of stress, the sinuses, ears and eyes, lungs, spine, kidneys, bladder, urethra, hips, knees, digestive system, reproductive organs and lymphatic system. By concentrating on these areas with deep pressure, any blockages can be located. If there is "stress" or a blockage, the therapist can normally feel crystal-like particles under the skin. If this is the case, the therapist will continue applying pressure until the crystal-like particles have disappeared. The client may initially feel discomfort, but after the session most feel revitalized and renewed. Reflexology, like other hands-on therapies, should be incorporated into the lifestyle. How often depends upon each individual, although at least monthly maintenance is suggested. Although the feet are connected to all the vital organs in the body, most reflexologists will not diagnose a critical illness.

Shiatsu Massage

Shiatsu in translation means "finger pressure." Like reflexology, it relaxes and helps heal the body through pressure points located on different points (acupoints) all over the body. Once again, these points are located on meridian lines. Unlike reflexology, which basically just uses the pressure of the fingers and thumbs, Shiatsu also applies pressure to larger areas using the palms, elbows and even the knees and feet. Usually in a Shiatsu session, the therapist will also use some stretching techniques. Unlike traditional massage, which tries to relax the muscles, the goal of Shiatsu is to ensure the constant flowing of positive Qi around the body. This in turn enables the body to help heal itself. It also releases physical and emotional tension, creating balance in both the body and mind. Shiatsu massage normally takes one hour.

Reiki

Recently Reiki (Ray-Key), an ancient Eastern therapy has gained recognition in the West to aid in harmonizing all aspects – mental, physical and spiritual – of the person. During a Reiki treatment, the healing energy is channeled through the Reiki practitioner and into the client. It is important to note that the Reiki therapist is channeling a "universal energy" – not his or her own energy. Similarities can be seen in the philosophy of Reiki and that of the scientific premise that everything – both solid and liquid, both visible and invisible, mind and matter – is all an accumulation of different forms of energy. Therefore, in order to relieve stress related problems, Reiki works on all energy levels – the physical, emotional, mental and spiritual. The theory is that the problem lies in one of these energy levels. The energy levels are treated holistically because they are connected to each other and what affects one, will at some point, affect the other. Both the cause and the symptom of the disease are treated. The Reiki therapist does not actually touch the body, but skims the surface of the body channeling this universal energy. Reiki sessions vary in length, depending upon each individual.

" I wish that every human life might be pure transparent freedom. "

SIMONE DE BEAUVOIR, 20TH CENTURY FRENCH PHILOSOPHER AND WRITER

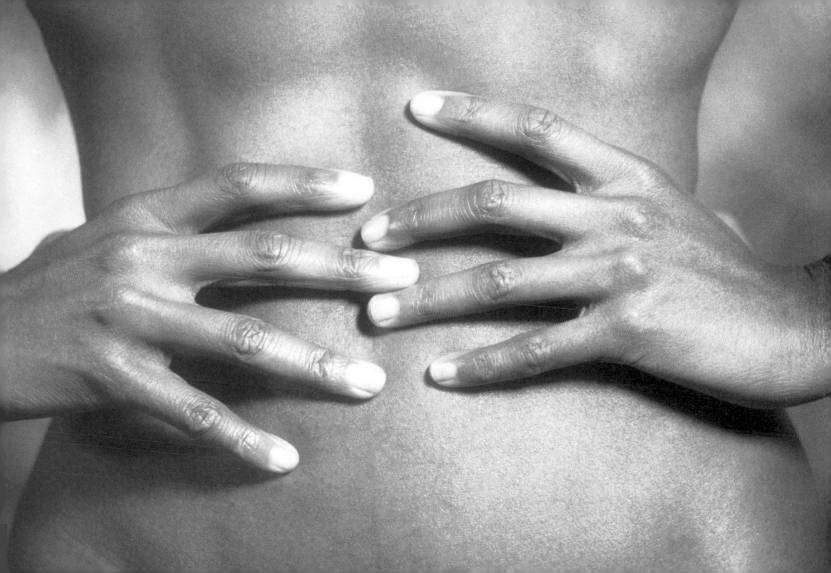

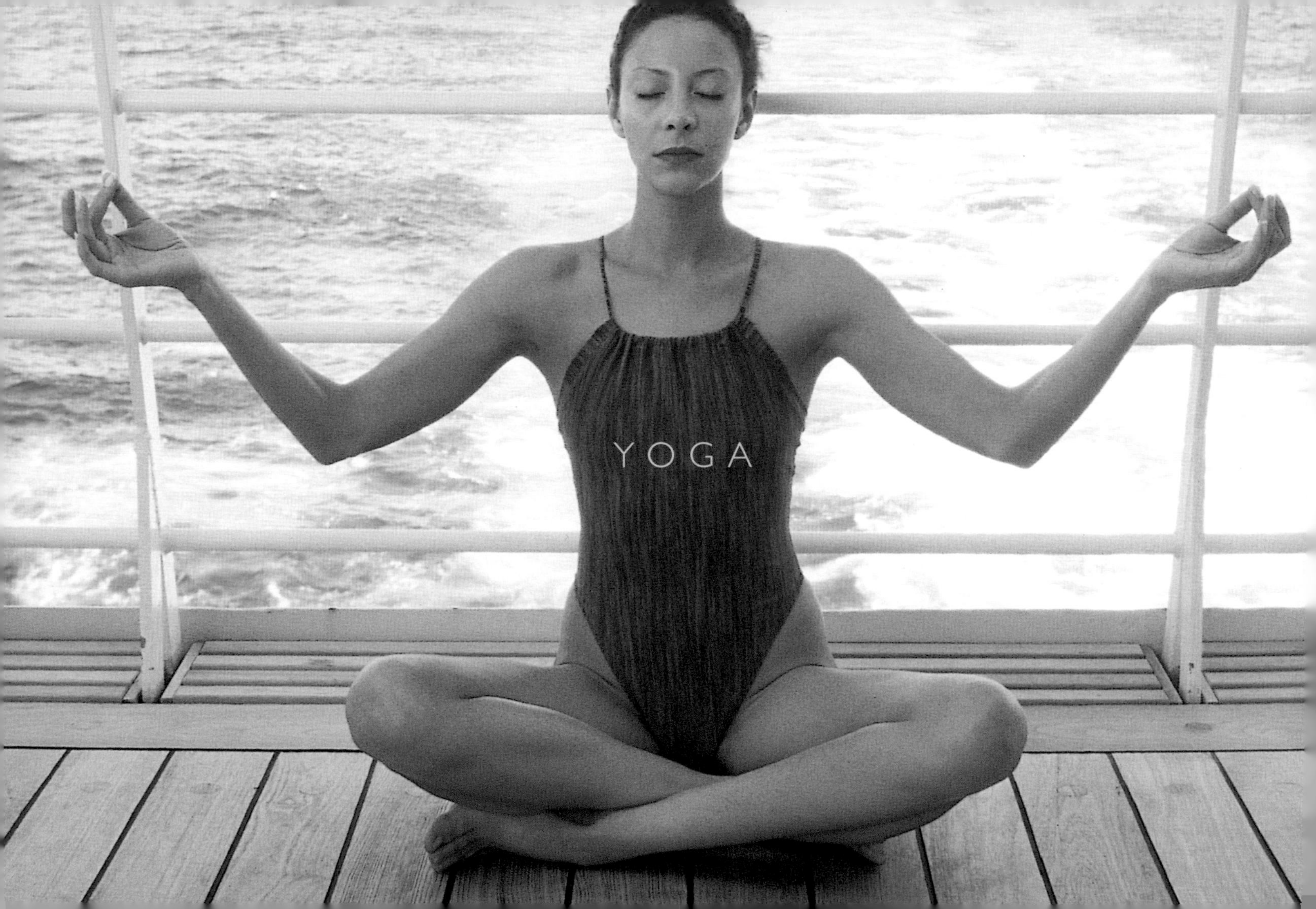
YOGA

Yoga is a sanskrit word meaning "spiritual union," and with this in mind, its origins have a divine purpose — to evoke spiritual awareness. The first written accounts of the spiritual processes of yoga are found in "the Vedas," ancient Sanskrit scriptures. Yoga, in this original sense, is a "path" that helps pacify the mind, allowing intense concentration. Within this intense concentration, spiritual awareness can be achieved.

The Yoga practice that has been made popular in the west is "Hatha" Yoga, which uses physical health and well being as the pathway to inner balance and spiritual awareness. Breathing during a Hatha Yoga class is part of the practice. Like abdominal breathing on page 32, the breath is deliberate and has a purpose. It should be in harmony with your physical movements during the Yoga class. Inhaled air, for the ancient Yoga masters contained "*prana*," an invisible force that inspires and renews. These wise old masters, witnessed the influence each breath had on every vital organ of their body. A deep, long breath helps to slow the blood pressure and heart rate. It also has a calming effect on the mind.

During a Hatha Yoga session, the instructor will start with light stretching and breathing exercises before asking you to attempt some of the more intricate poses. Each session lasts 1-2 hours and, regularly practiced, will make a huge difference to your state of mind. What many people do not realize is that the pain you feel during a session is an indication of tension in that area. During a session, you should note any discomfort * (which you are bound to feel if just a beginner) and try not to be distracted by it. After practicing Yoga, you should notice that these areas of tension are relieved, evoking a feeling of inner calm and balance during the course of the day. Do not be scared to ask your instructor to help you with a certain position, and if you are having a lot of difficulty, then simply do not do it.

Some different Yoga practices include: KARMA YOGA which achieves union through service and right action; MANTRA YOGA which finds this union through speech and sound, and KUNDALINI YOGA which focuses on the chakras of the body. There are many more Yoga disciplines all of which have the same goal in mind.

* If you do feel discomfort, tell your instructor. She or he may help ease you into a position or recommend you try a more basic exercise.

"I like being unconventional."

FLORENCE GRIFFITH JOYNER, 20TH CENTURY AMERICAN TRACK ATHLETE

Time to Meditate

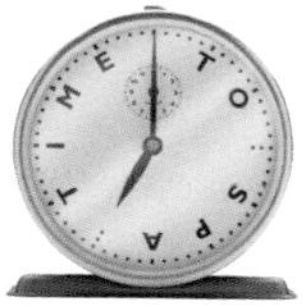
TIME TO SPA

"There is no purifier like knowledge in this world: time makes man find himself in his heart."

BHAGAVADGITA, "THE SONG OF GOD," AUTHOR UNKNOWN

An ancient technique, meditation was revived in the second half of the twentieth century and is a method for centering yourself, re-balancing your mind and reconnecting with the essential. It also expands your ability to concentrate, can help lower blood pressure, help reduce stress-related anxiety and can assist any creative process. Most people think meditation is another Eastern influence. The truth is that all cultures have used meditation throughout the ages. In the West, the early monks in monasteries found solace through chanting hymns. Similarly, Eastern meditation often includes the chanting of a mantra. Today, meditation is used by many people to help evoke peace of mind and to help spark creativity. The mind is concentrating on "nothing" which is a great art in itself. To think of nothing is perhaps the most difficult thing any mind can accomplish. It is a primordial experience that can really assist in both physical and emotional well being. To follow is an example of a meditation, which may help guide you into the meditative "alpha" state of mind, which is a zone of "unaware awareness." It is a state of complete relaxation achieved just before a deep sleep.

Tips: If this is your first meditation, then don't expect too much. Try to last for ten minutes. If you cannot focus then try to use taped meditation scripts or relaxation music. **Make sure you are comfortable, preferably in the Lotus position** upon a soft cushion. **Alternatively, you can sit in a chair or lie down.** Your first challenge will be to stay awake. Remember you want to be relaxed, but you also want to be extremely aware. **The key is to concentrate. Do not be put off if you do not succeed immediately. Just practice.** Wear comfortable loose or stretchy clothing and find your position.

*The Lotus position is the most widely known Yoga position. This position is often too difficult for beginners to achieve comfortably. Simply cross your legs until the Lotus position is comfortable for you.

THE SANCTUARY MEDITATION

To begin, sit in the Lotus position, or other comfortable position, and practice abdominal breaths. Slowly, breathe in through your nose. Each time you breathe in, imagine the oxygen circulating around your body. Breathe out through your nose, each time imagining all your worries, aches, pains and fears leaving you. Continue breathing this way, and as you become more relaxed, divert your attention to a deep, quiet place inside with every exhalation. The Sanctuary meditation is not focused upon any particular "goal" except sheer relaxation. Meditations can focus upon goals. For example, if you want to expand your creativity, you could imagine yourself in your "creative room" and create a space that has everything in it that would keep you occupied. Other meditations may focus upon psychological pain or fear.

Imagine you are opening a door which leads to a pathway in nature's garden. You start walking and with every step you are going deeper and deeper into your own sanctuary. With every step you take, you feel lighter, more energized, more peaceful and more centered. As you are walking, you take a look around and notice the beauty of this garden. This is your inner sanctuary. This is a reflection of you. Take a few moments to see, feel, experience and create it. Does it have a pond? Are there animals? Is it sunny and warm or a crisp bright winter's morning? Perhaps it is the beach or a mountain top. Take a few moments to create it. Lie in the grass, swim in the pond, rest against a tree. Draw a picture. Play in this sanctuary for as long as you like before you turn back and return to the path, back to the doorway. As you leave, take one last look at this beautiful place. This is your inner sanctuary and you can return and re-create it as often as you like.

" I am in love with moistness. "

GEORGE ELIOT, 19TH CENTURY ENGLISH WRITER

8

Time for Water

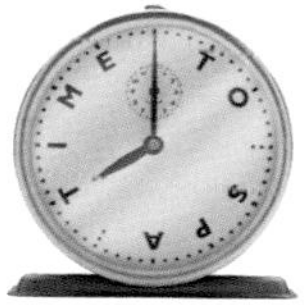
TIME TO SPA

What is this sense of well-being that pervades our being at the beach? What is that sensation of complete peace when you submerge your entire body and head underwater so that all you can hear are echoes reverberating in your mind? Is it a memory of the warmth of the womb, or just the wonder of this see-through liquid that can never be still? Thales, the first Greek philosopher (550BCE), believed that water was the "source of life." He noted that everything moist is alive, and everything dry is inanimate. He was not so wrong. Water is vital for life and many poems and songs have been inspired by its depths. It is a mystery. Our eyes and minds are hypnotized as we try to follow a wave to its destruction. And what about the many voices it has? Sometimes it whispers like a lover. Other times it roars like thunder. And it's aroma—a mixture of salt, sand, fish and seaweed. Water has held us captivated forever and, although scientists can reduce it to H_2O and trace elements, it's mysterious quality remains intact and undiscovered.

" The present moment is a powerful goddess. "

JOHANN WOLFGANG GOETHE, 18TH / 19TH CENTURY GERMAN WRITER

The science of seawater. Seawater is full of trace elements and minerals which help to maintain a healthy thyroid and a healthy circulation. This combined with a beautiful sunny day is irresistible and healthful to mind, body and soul.

Seaweed Therapies

Seaweed is a rich form of mineral and trace elements. It has an important job – to produce a substantial amount of oxygen for the earth. It is rich in chlorophyll, iodine and vitamins. Some marine specialists think that seaweed has anti-aging properties, and can help the immune system fight against the effects of pollution. The best part is that the benefits of seaweed can be absorbed through the body when used in wraps or baths.

Seaweed Wraps

These can be pure seaweed or a mixture of seaweed with other natural ingredients that aid detoxification and relaxation. As an example, Elemis combines pure seaweed extracts with the power of aromatherapy. The mixture remineralizes, detoxifies, and awakens the skin. The treatment smells and feels delicious. The body is cleansed with an astringent before being covered by the thick, green mixture and wrapped in a cocoon. It feels invigorating and every substance used in the mixture can be absorbed by the skin improving vitality and health.

Thalassotherapy Pools

Thalassotherapy pools are a twentieth century invention and have been modeled upon natural bubbling mineral spas combined with the healing effects of seawater. Quite simply, the thalassotherapy pool is heated to body temperature eliminating the "cold water shock." There are multiple jet stations located around the pool, each massaging a different location on the body. When in the pool you should start at the jet station that massages the soles of the feet and move around until you have reached the last station that massages the back of the neck. Most pools also have a floatation area where you can lay upon the water while powerful jets support you and massage the back of your body. There may also be powerful water showers that pour gallons of water upon your neck and shoulders. Thalassotherapy is more than a "swimming pool" or a bubbling jacuzzi. It has therapeutic qualities that can help ease arthritic pain, sore joints or pulled muscles; improving sluggish circulations and improving the metabolism.

Hydrotherapy Spa Baths

Unlike the Thalassotherapy Bath, the Hydrotherapy Spa Bath uses fresh water in a private bath. Like the Thalassotherapy Pool it has high pressure jets placed in different locations, which massage pressure points all over the body. Different potions can be added to the bath, including but not limited to, dried seaweed, aromatherapy bath oils, milk baths, essential oils and foaming baths.

Thalassotherapy is more than a " swimming pool " or a bubbling jacuzzi.

THE WONDER OF WATER

Natural Mineral Springs

Our Roman ancestors soothed sore joints with a lavish dip in a Roman Bath. Ingeniously designed, the Roman Bath was built upon natural bubbling mineral springs found in various locations all over the Empire. Still "bubbling" today, the Roman Bath found in Bath, England was a favorite watering hole of many fine, young Romans.

The Fountain Of Youth

When Ponce De Leon discovered the Land of Flowers "Florida," he also stumbled upon the Fountain of Eternal Youth. He was convinced that this holy water would make time stand still. Alas he was mistaken. Good try though.

British Spa Towns

The Victorians frequented Spa Towns for a medicinal sip and dip in the natural spring water—for health reasons of course. During the spring and summer, the aristocracy would spend weeks bathing mind, body and soul in these natural pools.

The Water at Lourdes

Every year thousands of people surrender mind, body and soul to the healing water at Lourdes, France. Ever since the Virgin Mother was seen in a vision, the once secluded river now attracts thousands of tourists.

Create your own holy dip.

If you don't have time to dip your aching body into a Thalassotherapy pool or the water at Lourdes, use the healing power of water that flows from your own faucets. Draw a bath. But before you do, create some spa ambiance.

1

Put on some soothing music.
Perhaps the sounds of the ocean or a rhapsodic arrangement
of violins, harps and guitars—music that will not intrude upon
your spa experience like an unwelcome guest.

2

Turn out the lights, light some candles. Fire—another great
primordial mystery never ceases to fascinate the mind with
dancing flames. Light some aromatic burners.
Use essences like lavender and chamomile to help relax your mind.

3

Draw your bath and pour
a few drops of your favorite essential oils,
foaming bath, herbs or seaweed.
Slide in and get lost in your own world.

"She was built with curves like the hull of a racing yacht, and you missed none of it with that wool jersey." ERNEST HEMINGWAY, 20TH CENTURY AMERICAN WRITER

9 Time for Exercise

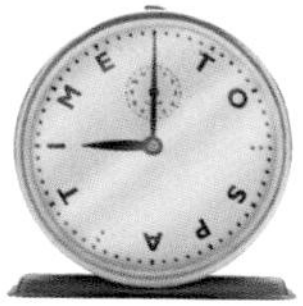

What if you hate the thought of exercise? There's still no excuse to succumb to the couch and practice the art of being a potato. Exercise is not supposed to be a chore. It's supposed to naturally occur in your life. Just think. Two thousand years ago everything was done manually. Most people would build their own homes and pull their own water from a well. Food was planted and picked. The most common mode of transportation was the "foot" and people would walk hundreds of miles to pilgrimage sites every Spring. When ancient heroes did sail the seas in their magnificent ships, they were manually driven using the North Star as the compass and the hard work of sailors. With the constant progress of technology, we are at risk of losing touch with the body's natural need to move and sweat. If you hate the thought of going to a gymnasium then that's okay. There are plenty of other things you can do.

"We are astonished at thought, but sensation is equally wonderful.

Voltaire, 17th / 18th Century Philosopher, Writer and Historian

Dancing What do you think aerobics is? Dance your way through the days you feel like eating ice cream and jelly. If you go to night clubs, inhabit the center of the floor. As long as you keep up your pace, dancing will burn up as much calories as an aerobics class—between 375 and 750 calories per hour.

Belly Dancing This Eastern dance is becoming quite popular and there are lots of classes available—it does wonders for your belly! Not quite as calorie burning or cardiovascular as aerobics, but it really helps to tone. If you keep it up for an hour you will probably burn between 250 and 450 calories per hour.

Rowing Need to firm your shoulders and chest? Hire a rowing boat and take a loved one for a romantic trip down the river. It's great fun and great exercise and you will burn up between 600-1050 calories per hour.

Mountain Climbing Not for the faint hearted. Mountain climbing can be dangerous and exciting, as well as a great cardiovascular and muscular activity. You can burn between 600 to 1050 calories per hour.

Skiing If you live near snow capped mountains during the winter, take advantage and ski away your excess energy and between 700-1200 calories per hour.

Swimming Beware—floating does not count! If you want to employ a daily swim to keep yourself trim, then make sure you do some energetic laps for at least half an hour at a time. You'll burn between 400 and 900 calories per hour.

Cycling Cycling is a wonderful cardiovascular activity. Again, if you cycle half an hour every day you'll look and feel fitter. Ultimately, you should aim to cycle 40 to 50 miles per week if cycling is your only form of exercise. Depending on how fast you pace yourself, you can burn between 450 and 1125 calories per hour while cycling. Not only that, you get to breathe some fresh air.

Walking This must be "intentional" walking. Keep your head high, swing your arms freely and clench your buttock muscles while you walk. Take big strides and breathe deeply. If you walk half an hour per day you will feel revitalized and energized. Walking will burn between 300-450 calories per hour.

Jogging A great cardiovascular exercise. Just make sure you wear good jogging shoes to protect your knees if you jog on concrete. Again, jogging can burn from 450 to 1125 calories per hour.

In-line Skating Great fun and great exercise. Once you start skating you'll burn off lots of calories and sweat away lots of toxins. Besides learning the art of balance, you will burn between 450-750 calories per hour.

Yoga Yoga is wonderful for stretching the limbs, massaging the internal organs and relaxing through the perfect breath. Breathing oxygenates the body which helps to speed up the metabolism. (see page 50) You will burn 250-450 calories per hour, depending upon the level of difficulty.

ASSESS YOUR CARDIOVASCULAR GOALS

First of all work out your maximum heart rate (MHR) using this formula: 220 MINUS AGE. For example if you are 55 years old your MHR is 165 beats per minute. Check your resting heart rate (RHR). To do this simply take your pulse for a full minute. For best results take this first thing in the morning before you get out of bed.

Next determine your heart rate reserve (HRR). To do this subtract the resting heart rate from the maximum heart rate. For example if your resting heart rate is 65 beats per minute and your maximum heart rate is 165 beats per minute then your HRR is 100 beats per minute.

Finally, determine the beats per minute you want to achieve for a cardiovascular work out. You can determine a work out at 50% to 85% of the HRR. To do this, all you have to do is work out 85% of HRR (100 bpm) and then add the resting heart rate.

Using the formulas above that would be: 100 x 85% + 65. Your cardiovascular goal would then be 150 bpm.

Note: If you do not work out, do not exert yourself. 85% of your HRR is the type of workout a trained person would undergo. If you are a beginner, start your work out at 50% HRR for the first four to six weeks before you start exerting yourself more. You should keep the exercise going for 20-30 minutes at least and slowly increase the time to 45-60 minutes. Realistically cardiovascular activity should be done at least four times per week. We recommend you consult your doctor before starting an exercise program.

"The moment of change is the only poem.

ADRIENNE RICH, 20TH CENTURY AMERICAN POET

1234567891 0

Changing the Face of Time

We all have changing faces. Every second denotes change. It's part of the beauty of life. Change cannot be fought and should be embraced as the ultimate nature of the world.

Since time immemorial the ancient myths tell us of those heroes and heroines who sought eternal youth. Gilgamesh, the Sumerian "Demi-God," who ruled in a city in ancient Mesopotamia 4700 years ago, inspired the poem "Epic of Gilgamesh." Originally written in Cuneiform, it describes his quest to achieve immortality. When his search failed, he desperately tried to capture the magical formula of eternal youth. Alas, after a valiant struggle with the forces of nature, he lost grasp of this too and finally accepted his fate as the mortal demi-god that he was!

The art of growing older is rooted in today's state of mind, our attitude and in the lifestyle we lead.

This is one of many similar myths that indicate the human instinct to post-pone change and delay the years. So often we translate youth as being one's physical appearance alone but, what is more important, is one's state of mind – one's attitude toward life and one's self awareness. Physical beauty, without these other qualities, is wasted because we are as beautiful as we perceive ourselves to be – not as we look to others. The key then to true beauty is self awareness, self acceptance and, most importantly, how well we enjoy life.

We are born with certain unchangeable "face" facts, like bone structure, skin tone, the color of our eyes, the shape of the mouth. **But, the invisible beauty – t he glow in a smile, the sparkle of the eyes, the rosy hue on a cheek – these are all dependent upon well being.**

"Life gives you the face
you have at twenty;
it's up to you to merit the
face you have at fifty.

Coco Chanel, 19th / 20th Century French Couturiere

Skin. The largest organ of your body. The protector of an interior world. Your interior world. Impermeable, it's like an exit-only window that banishes toxins out of little portholes in your skin. It is a fortress. A temple. A beautiful miracle.

Think of your skin as a looking glass that reveals the interior of your mind and body. Mental stress, bad diet, sleepless nights, pollution and general self neglect are all reflected in the surface of your skin with a dull complexion, blemishes and/or premature lines. With this in mind, when you think about caring for your skin, you should be thinking about caring for your essential organs and focusing upon creating a lifestyle that is congenial with well being. Many beauty experts distinguish between two types of aging – extrinsic aging and intrinsic aging. Intrinsic aging is the aging from within. It is natural aging. It is a result of time. Forty years of smiling and laughing will leave those happy days imprinted on your skin because the processes of renewal slow down with time. On the other hand extrinsic aging is caused from exterior forces. Spending too much time in the sun; pollutants in the atmosphere; smoking; drinking alcohol; excessive stress; eating food that is difficult to digest (junk foods, artificial foods, red meat) ; an unhealthy lifestyle. Extrinsic aging is the only aging anyone should be concerned about, because it is in our control and it is very much the result of lifestyle.

Skin Function

Your skin is a protector and barrier against moisture loss. It prevents bacteria entering the body. It helps to regulate the temperature via the sweat glands. It is self-caring, secreting sebum to keep the skin soft and pliable. It also has an excretory function, ridding the body of toxins. The skin is a sensory system, which is connected to the nervous system. Anxiety, depression and stress are all reflected within the skin.

Food for Skin

You are what you eat—a trite cliché perhaps, yet undeniably wise. For a healthy skin and body, a variety of carbohydrates, fat, protein, vitamins, minerals and water should be included in the daily diet. It is the foods rich in vitamins and minerals that we term as skin food. These are generally your fresh fruit and vegetables. These foods with vitamin A, E and C, act as anti-oxidants for the skin and body by helping to stabilize the "free radicals" that naturally form in the body. Free radicals are unstable molecules which have incomplete charges. They try to complete themselves by robbing the charges from another molecule. This in turn has a damaging effect to cells in the body. Anti-oxidant foods and treatments promote cell longevity and reduce risk of cell damage by attaching themselves to free radicals and "completing" them before they attack internal molecules. Carotene (a high easy-to-find source of vitamin A) can be found in oranges, carrots, mangoes and dark green leafy veggies. Remember, fresh food is always better than processed or pre-cooked food, because the nutrients will be at their optimum level.

Organic Food

There is a food war going on right now between farmers who grow organically and farmers who prefer conventional methods. The basic difference between organic and conventional farming methods is that organic food is grown without the use of pesticides and artificial chemicals. Advocates of organic farming state that pesticides can be harmful to health and according to the Environmental Protection Agency, more than 107 different active ingredients in pesticides are known or probable carcinogens. Symptoms like tension, anxiety, insomnia, emotional instability, increased heart rate, breathing difficulties and even vomiting have been documented as being pesticide related illnesses in some cases. Organic food availability is growing throughout the world and although it is in some cases double the price of conventional food, it could help promote quality of life and a radiant skin.[3]

"Age is something that doesn't matter, unless you are a cheese."

BILLIE BURKE, 19TH / 20TH CENTURY AMERICAN ACTRESS

Cleansing

Our philosophy is to cleanse using natural cleansers which is why Elemis products were created. Your skin is completely natural and therefore the cleansing lotions used should be gentle and non-abrasive. This means that the extracts that have been used within the cleanser should be grown ensuring optimum health to each plant. An alternative to a creamy cleanser is a foaming wash. These cleansers create a soapy lather without stripping away the sebum.

Toning

The perfect toner is just a light, non-alcoholic astringent that removes the cleanser and closes the pores. For those that cleanse with a lathering wash instead, a flower water mist can take the place of the toner.

Moisturizing

Beauty experts agree that moisturizing is extremely important for all skin types and all ages. It acts as a buffer between your skin and the environment. Aromatic moisturizers containing plant essential oils and products containing palmisomes (a natural plant agent that helps transport nutrients to the skin) can be absorbed by the skin into the blood stream. One of the newest technological advances for natural skin care is the advent of "Absolute" extraction. Absolutes are the most concentrated form of active essential oils that can be extracted from the petals of flowers. As an example it takes eight million jasmine blossoms to create one kilo of Absolutes. It is a highly expensive technology, but it guarantees that the product will be active and have the ability to be absorbed by the skin. Presently, Elemis is the only skin care range using this technology.

Anti-Aging Creams

The more packed with natural anti-oxidants, palmisomes and vitamins, the more nutrients your moisturizer will provide for your skin. Remember your skin care program is only part of an entire lifestyle that should be geared toward wellbeing. Rich moisturizers will be of little help to skin that is not supported through diet, exercise and stress reducing techniques. As part of your skin care program, anti-aging creams are like the icing on a delicious cake. Yum!

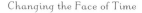

Soap mythology. According to beauty experts, soap is the first beauty item to banish from all bathroom cabinets. Instead of cleansing the skin of impurities, it strips it of the lipid barrier, which helps keep the skin supple and moist. In oily skins the sebum is completely cleansed away. This famine of sebum is communicated to the brain, which then provides more oil to the skin. Ironically, in this case, stripping away the oils only serves to make the skin even oilier. Soap has an adverse effect on skin for one reason. It is alkaline (some are as high as a pH 12) and skin is acidic (4.5-5.5).

Eye Creams

The skin around the eye and neck area is much more delicate and more prone to loss of elasticity. This is not a myth. The skin is much thinner which is why heavy creams around the eyes can cause puffiness. Special, lighter creams are therefore produced to help moisturize these fragile areas.

Skin Scrubs

Your skin is like the moon. It renews itself completely every 28 or so days. Scrubs with tiny granules help this natural exfoliating process by letting the new healthy skin emerge. As the skin ages, this process of renewal slows down and using an exfoliator more regularly can support the skin. Once again, you want to be wise when shopping – some scrubs use synthetic ingredients that can scratch the skin. Your skin scrub should contain natural abrasive particles, like Diatomaceous Phytoplankton, a naturally crushed earthy particle found on the ocean floor, combined with other natural emollients and plant essences. Most therapists recommend using a skin scrub once or twice a week.

Hiding Behind a Mask

It's healthy to "don a mask" once a week during a spa date with yourself. There are different masks but basically they have two focused missions. The first is deep cleansing. After using your scrub, the mask will help to penetrate into the pores and withdraw any impurities before they turn into blemishes. The second mission is deep, intensive moisturizing and lifting. These masks should be rich with aromatic oils that help to relax and de-stress the skin.

Treatment Creams

After an illness, or if you are just completely overworked, your skin will probably need a boost. This is because all your energy is being used for recovery and not for maintenance. Obviously this is your body's way of curing itself, but it tends to leave your skin and your hair dull and lifeless. At these times, don't hesitate to use booster creams to help pick your skin up. Booster creams will include vitamins like C, D, E and "Absolutes." Skin boosters, when used too often, may be too rich. Just keep some handy for those run down days.

"It seems necessary to completely shed the old skin before the new, brighter, stronger, more beautiful one can emerge... I never thought I'd be getting my life lesson from a snake!"

JULIA RIDGE, 20TH CENTURY AMERICAN ATHLETE, ACTRESS AND WRITER

THE AGING SUN

The Sun – so beautiful and healthful, yet so dangerous. It is good and evil rolled into a fireball in the sky. Good because it feels so good; making plants grow; nourishing your body. It lures you to strip down to a bikini or trunks and surrender. Evil because it is too powerful for us, burning those who dare block its path for more than an hour. Never the less, like obsessed lovers, we return to the beaches with our bodies stretched upon the sand in complete abandonment, beckoning the treachery of her rays. The result isn't so poetic with premature aging, uneven skin pigmentation, burns and worst of all, skin cancer, being a possible end result.

Sun Tips: Avoid sun bathing! **If you do sunbathe, do it in the early morning for half an hour to an hour.** Paler skins should use an SPF of 30 or more. **Darker skins still need protection from the sun and should still cover the body and use a minimum of SPF 15.** Use one ounce or the equivalent of 2 tablespoons of sunscreen for the average adult body. **Do not scrimp, spread it generously.**

" *In the Primordial Age Woman Was Once the Sun!* "

RAICHO HIRATSUKA, 19TH / 20TH CENTURY JAPANESE WRITER

Tell Tale Sun Stressed Signs

Damaged facial skin looks like thick leather with deeply etched lines. This result does not occur over night. It is the result of years of sun abuse. If the skin reaches this damaged stage, the possibility of sun damage reversal by preventative measures is weakened. On the other hand, for those of you who do sun bathe and do not have such vivid implications of sun damage, the chances are you can reverse the effects of sun damage and prevent the results from appearing on your face. Dr. Deborah Sarnoff, Assistant Clinical Professor at New York University and private practicing dermatologist in New York, says that while some skin appears undamaged "it may be hidden deeply under the skin's immediate surface and can only be seen by an ultraviolet light." Under this light, "even a perfect skin will reveal freckles and uneven pigments under the skin's surface and excess sun also swells the capillaries and broadens the pores. It's a huge price to pay for a golden tan."

Dr. Sarnoff noted that in a test on sun damaged skin, the participants who agreed to be sun savvy by covering themselves with a hat, clothing that covered the body and who used sun screen and moisturizer regularly, noticed a reversal of sun damage.

The Truth About Ultra Violet (UV) A, B and C

Dr. Sarnoff states that UVA is the longest radiation wave. It is not filtered by the ozone and strikes the earth 150 times more than UVB. It does not burn but penetrates the dermis and is the culprit of wrinkles and leathery skin. It lowers immunity. UVB is the medium radiation wave length. It is not completely filtered by the ozone. It burns the skin and could cause damage to the DNA, altering the skin cells' function. Excessive damage could lead to skin cancer. UVC is the shortest wave length. It is high energy radiation that has the potential to damage the skin but at this time the ozone absorbs it completely. However, ecologists say that if the ozone should cease to be a fortress because of pollution (airplanes, cars, factories, aerosol cans etc.) then this too could be a problem in the future.

We hope that "Time to Spa" will inspire you on your quest for well being. As society becomes more technical, the need for simple pleasures that evoke tranquility and peace of mind becomes more urgent. It is our hope that you don't think of "spa" treatments, like massage and aromatherapy as indulgences or treats. Think of them as part of your lifestyle. It's time to spa.

www.timetospa.com

If you would like an Elemis product catalog please call 1-800-423-5293 or 1-800-772-7911. Visit us on the web: www.timetospa.com
Send us an email: steiner@steinerleisure.com or write us at: 770 South Dixie Highway, Suite 200, Coral Gables, Florida 33146

NOTES

1) Hoeger and Hoeger. *Principles and Labs for Fitness and Wellness.* Pages 203-204. 5th Ed. New York

2) *Smoking Cravings are Reduced by Self Massage.* Pages 28-32. Preventative Medicine, 1999

3) Wild Oats Market. *Organic Power.* Pages 7-8. Printed by Wild Oats Market

BIBLIOGRAPHY

Dawes, Nigel, *Shiatsu for Beginners.* California: Prima Publishing, 1995

Hoeger and Hoeger. *Principles and Labs for Fitness and Wellness.* 5th Ed. New York: Morton Publishing Company, 1999

Hoffman, David. *The Complete Illustrated Holistic Herbal.* Boston: Element Books Limited, 1996

Isaacson, Cheryl. *Yoga Step by Step.* London: Thorsons, 1990

Iyengar, BKS. *Light on Yoga.* New York: Schocken Books, 1979

QUOTES

Pages 5, 12, 32, 36, 38, 42, 48, 52, 74, 77, 80, 83 and 85. *The Quotable Woman.* Philadelphia: Running Press, 1991

Pages 19, 26, 28, 54, 61, 66 and 88. *The International Thesaurus of Quotations.* New York: Harper Perennial, 1996

Pages 20 and 24. *Cassell Dictionary of Contemporary Quotations.* London: Cassell, 1998

"To see a world in a grain of sand and a heaven in a wild flower, hold infinity in the palm of your hand and eternity in an hour."

WILLIAM BLAKE, 18TH / 19TH CENTURY BRITISH POET

...tick...tock...tick...tock...tick...tock...tick...tock...tick...tock...tick...tock...tick...tock...tick...